*One Eye and a Measuring Rod*

# ONE EYE AND A MEASURING ROD

Poems by

John L'Heureux

NEW YORK
The Macmillan Company
Collier-Macmillan Limited
LONDON

ACKNOWLEDGMENTS

Cummings quotation on p. ix copyright 1926 by Horace Liveright; copyright © 1954 by E. E. Cummings. Reprinted from *Poems 1923-1954* by E. E. Cummings by permission of Harcourt, Brace & World, Inc.

"The Gift," "The Bargain," "Brother Jordan's Fox," "The Prince Mourns His Love," "A Pleasing Fragrance" first appeared in *Atlantic Monthly*.

"The Startled Flower," "The Gift," "Testimonial: The Dog of Mrs. Hammonton," and "Thrasher" reprinted with permission of The Macmillan Company from *Picnic in Babylon* by John L'Heureux. Copyright © John L'Heureux, S.J., 1967.

Other poems originally appeared in *America, Beloit Poetry Journal, Bogus, Catholic World, Critic, Harper's, Motive, Quarterly Review of Literature, Stimulus, The Month* (London), *Woodstock Letters*.

Library of Congress Catalog Card Number: 68-23636

First Printing

The Macmillan Company, New York
Collier-Macmillan Canada Ltd., Toronto, Ontario
Printed in the United States of America

Str 495/248/3/19/69

FOR *Regina*

*"there is no hunger
like the taste of you"*

# Contents

*(While you and I have lips and voices which
are for kissing and to sing with
who cares if some oneeyed son of a bitch
invents an instrument to measure Spring with?*

e. e. cummings

# I. Some Praise and
a Little Blame

## BROTHER JORDAN'S FOX

THE FOX,
crippled, walks
on his knees. Cocks

fear no danger
from his broken anger.
Rabbits linger

in his presence.
He scents
quail and pheasants

to no purpose.
He must
like all of us

acknowledge law:
the iron jaws
that took his forepaws

took his food.
His anguished blood
does him no good,

he lives by pity
and the brief rarity
of our charity.

The taste
of meat is daily spiced
with a past

he can no longer
shape to his hunger
or to that stronger

will to love.
He must live
forgiving that we give

him life. His pride
in that golden hide
of his provides

him nothing. He
knows it well, pretends we
do not see

without us he would die.
Just such a lie
burnishes our copper eyes.

## FABRICATION

WHEN I WOKE THE MORNING
at a sunless and uncivil hour
(4:45 A.M.)

those crazy birds
had not yet tuned
for matins.

I gave them pitch
warned the dewy worms go under
spied death gliding

back to his bone orchard.
I gave you this first time
the morning.

I made it. I woke it.
That bird singing
is my soul's surprise.

Sunrise is a lovelong
giving
to learn ourselves.

## THE STARTLED FLOWER

THE BABY KISSES FLOWERS.
I saw him.
What untaught harmony
he must shape

to chaos he will learn—
later—with the force
of time and tolerance.
He will hate flowers. But now

green anemones
are falling through the air,
Gregory; sea flowers
startled from their stems

by your soft kiss.
I touch your brow
that more than graceful flower
before it crumbles into dust.

# THE DIFFIDENT LADY

"where my heart should be
there is a ball of wool"
                    The D. L.

THAT SMALL ITCH
at the bare part
scratches my soul.

The form of your
bright mystery
unravelled

from a ball of wool
might, in time,
unwind your heart

and tighten about mine
stopping
that small itch

forever. I am afraid.
I wind the wool
upon my hand

holding
what virgin mystery:
the wool is living.

# THE GIFT

A DARNING EGG IS GOOD
    Of course
Though not exactly what you had in mind.
    He meant
    To give you
Something better. Growing up,
      He learned soon to ask for bread
      And take the offered scorpion.
Dusk settles;
It is all the same.

What from the first
    You loved
Was his outrageousness, you thought.
    After, you
    Were pleased
With his pitiful austere desires.
      He had grown up in desire, always.
      He woke at night, your name
Upon his lips.
You slept, smiling.

A darning egg is good
    For socks.
Lodgers make repairs that slip
    The mind.
    They must.
And you and he are lodgers—never

More than that—waiting to move on
In fear and insufficient wisdom
Groping to
A kind of truth,

A home, a you to love
For good
With talk and laughter and desire.
He meant
To give you
More than this. Much more. But
Take it anyway; you will remember
Him, his one last foolishness.
A darning egg
Is good, and serves.

## ABRAHAM

Nobody dies in this America.
They used to.
                    They did when Lincoln
split the rails of probability,
came loping out of Illinois to split
a dying land in two. Not peace

but the maiming ax. The heart
he cut out was his own, never wholly
mended, pieced together with a bland
prosperity where nobody dies any more.
Lincoln died.
                    They used to in America.
But now the civil heart lies still.

# REQUIEM FOR A YOUNG GOD

WHAT THEY SAY ABOUT YOU CHANGES
　　nothing. Too much is said
　　between the porch light
　　and the pale night's moon.

Creeping things have praised you,
　　beetles, worms, crickets.
　　The stiff-winged fowl
　　have clucked for you at dawn.

And shall I then forget? Sometimes
　　a love is not returned:
　　the borrowed key, the word
　　that only two can share

Is given to a third. It draws
　　the curtains over eyes.
　　Sometimes neglect: the door
　　not fixed because it creaked

Only in wet weather and who
　　can work in rain? Sometimes
　　fear casts a foreign shadow
　　on the blood and freezes.

Beloved, what they say about you
　　on the side porch, front porch,
　　in defiance of the crickets
　　and the sleepy winged fowl

Changes nothing. Blind captors
lead you to a comfortable
execution: tolerance. We
creeping things praise you.

## THE AFFAIR

Madame Lupinsky the tight-rope lady
boasted a balance that was incantation,

conjured from the sawdust stricken eyes.
No one breathed. No one said, oh look.

When Madame danced her thousand days
upon the line, continents caught flame.

Heaven gaped to see that tiny body
dancing light from incandescent wire,

raining stars upon the disbelieving dust
because she knew she could. She did.

She died one starless night, plunged
breathless from the wire to staring earth.

Some say it was a vision of the end.
Some say it never happened. Few believe.

Nonetheless, she died her way: balance
was a revelation, falling an act of grace.

*II. Facts*

## TESTIMONIAL: THE DOG OF MRS. HAMMONTON

"Nearly had to be put away, poor Daisy";
her fungus itch had all but made her crazy,
had made the beast a running sore with ears.

"I never could have put away our Daisy.
I suffered as she suffered, two whole years
of frenzied scratching at the frantic itch."

But Daisy's back is healed, the little bitch
boasts the fluffiest behind for blocks.
"The Lord should bless you for Sulfodox."

The Lord has blessed me for Sulfodox.
At better pet shops everywhere I am blessed.
That dog will never die. Be it confessed,

however, Mrs. Hammonton will die.
She—notwithstanding Sulfodox—will lie
beneath the daisies sealed in a wooden box

with pearls and worms twining in her breast.

## THE GRECIAN WINTER

AFTER THE FUNERAL
for her tenuous beliefs
she had noticed

honeycomb blooming
in the red meat
of the lion,

had made a pact
with maggots
for a good body

and a quick mind.
She tired
summer into fall

with her golden hand
blazing
in her tawny hair.

Every city fell
before her eyes
before her fabled breasts.

She laughed.
The honeycomb
behind her eyes

bloomed
sweet and fatal
as the lion's gut.

The bloom sustained her.
She lived
to see her pact fulfilled,

she died believing,
rich
in laughter and in love.

## FOREIGN TRAVEL

AT A SMALL CAFE IN VIENNA
six stern prophets ringed his table
(like a spy movie, like an apocalypse)
spelled him tomorrow.

Several virgins from the cinema
brought him German beer in tankards
(cradling them in their hairy arms).
He thought there must be some mistake.

There was no mistake.
There are never mistakes in Vienna
(except his being there, except his being)
and he drank his beer and frowned.

They were true prophets, they spoke doom.
True virgins, aching in their breasts.
(He sits in the cafe still, nine years since)
No one has seen him since that day.

Foreign travel is broadening
and less expensive than it seems.
(Sometimes of course one disappears)
Boil your water and carry soap.

And listen like Heidegger to what is not being said.

## THRASHER

WE ARE BETRAYED BY WHAT IS TRUE.

He leaped out from behind his face,
he always did, and said things
we don't say. Poor Thrasher.
Poor dim lodger. We grow to hate
the innocent we injure most;
the famished heart devours.

Winter dawned and settled in his eyes.
He stopped his leaping. When
all the guests went home at Christmas,
no one thought of Thrasher who sat
and hugged his toes. We were relieved
when at the end he took the hint
and passed on quietly. Rest in peace,

Thrasher,
you poor leaping toe-hugging innocent
slob.

## THE VISIT

THE DRAMA FAILS SOMETIMES. THEN HOODS
are thrown back and the truth emerges,
more variable than contrivance, more dangerous.

I too am prisoner of necessity. The dead
I never loved alive have not forgotten vigils
I refused to keep. You are not the only one.

The peacock's eye resting on my desk distracts,
does not defend me from the thick rain falling.

It was like this: I came into the room
and fixed my glass and failed to see, until
I stood there half out of my tee shirt, the cat
staring at me like a terror dream, commentary
on my soul. The crash of lightning was relief.
And then the flat rain tatting on the screen.
That cat was evil, nestled calmly at my back.

But now there is a cello sounding in the house
I know is empty. All the Capuchins have gone,
packed their flattened hoods and laughter,
left us our contrived simplicity a cat can shatter.

I scrounge for pieces, assemble the appalled
and ghostly quiet of my soul, a compromise with need.
The cello sounds. Strings of the mind are breaking.

But I refuse that drama. It is not the mind.
It is the cello wailing on the hurt wind
saying not "too late" but "you will never."

The peacock's eye is lying on the desk.
The cat is gone. Thrown out. It is unearthly
quiet. They are keeping vigil at the door.

## THE BERRY STAIN

MY SON, LITERAL CHILD OF IMAGINED
hours, said I love you to the garbage
man today. They know each other;
they have not thought of hating.

The garbage man shifted his pail
and dropped his banging scoop. John
stared and waited his reply—who
has, besides his wife, seven children

to absorb his time and loving.
"You be a good boy," he said
and shook his fist. John smiled.
They walked together to the truck.

The untaught genius of the tongue
is subtle poison. The belly warms
and death will find a smiling mouth.
The garbage man drove off, defeated.

## THE MUNICIPAL PARK

WE STONED THE WIDOW FIRST AND THEN
her child, ugly both of them. That
was our way of showing that the truth
alone has rights. Some protested

for a while, but later saw our wisdom.
She was a whore, you see. Her child,
allowed to live, would be a whore
as well, begetting whores. It was

a case of choosing some immediate
unpleasantness to spare our children
evil. The stones we hurled upon her
marked her grave until last April.

That was when the elders cleared away
debris to make a park and, as further
aid to virtue, put up a neat bronze
plaque to memorize her failings.

The plaque is on the birch tree
near the swings. That's all we have
of her, thank God—though rumor says
her child is still alive. He isn't.

# TIFFANY ALEXANDER

A DOG NOT BEAUTIFUL BUT BEAUTIFULLY
eccentric. A peculiar dog. Bizarre.
In the formal garden on the south-east
side, some funny sculptor chipped cement
to Pug-shape, footstool of an older
comfortable God. (Little he did depended
on the living) Frowning canine rage
from periwinkles, the Pug damns our sad
impermanence, commands us to become
cement disguises that we wear. He glowers.
(Placid eccentricity survives all weather)
Hello, you Pug, I shouted. The guests
turned modestly away. (The priest is mad)
Afternoon grew thin and chilly.

Returning home in rain, we met the dog.
A champagne yellow Willoughby Pug
(nine inches high, eighteen long)
came tritty trotting down the asphalt road
(fat little belly, collapsible face)
and—because he had two hundred years
of breeding—ignored me. Hello, you Pug.

Tiffany Alexander, Willoughby Pug,
ignored me. Damned yellow dog. Peculiar.
(We always know how best to strike our betters)
I wished him to the south-east garden
to his Chinese grandfather chipped

from cement. I wondered would he recognize
the flat black face, the eyes' tight
arrogance, the nostrils' curled disdain.
And then—for lack of half wit—he turned
back to me, tritty trotted back and twitched
his little dog-behind. Tiffany Alexander
(champagne yellow Willoughby aristocrat)
assured me which of us survived the weather.
He had not become the sorry face he wore.

# *JUDITH*

WE CANNOT YET BELIEVE YOUR PURPLE ELEGANCE
in weeds, drenched in his pagan blood—
Holofernes whose sin was love. He loved you.
Hollow woman, sensual and silent, mourning
golden in your hollow tabernacle, executing
God's stern will. He was reluctant to depart
his tent. You led him. Took his trusting
head. Stripped his bed of silken nets
and gold and jewels you had not seen before:
divine command consorting with your lust.

Reluctance. He delayed before his final kiss.
You knew he knew. You knew he sensed the knife
beneath his hair. He knew your consecrated
hate and still he loved. He died. Your people
call you blessed though they wonder when night
is heavy if you drape your stolen body, waiting,
with his silks and jewels. You too—reluctant
to depart. God's will is always contradictory.
Your beauty, Judith, your triumphant head,
rejoices the despairing love of saints.

## FOUNDLING

IN THE MIDDLE
of the conversation—
not breaking
his voice's stride—
he walked
to the corner
and stood there
facing the wall.
He was always strange.

At age one
he sat upon
the Bishop's lap
and terrified that saint
with gas.
Growing up
he ate peanutbutter
sandwiches
when all the rest of us
had porkchops.
He never tortured snakes.
Everywhere
he smelled, faintly,
corruption.
He grew confused,
discovered happiness
was just a myth
like meaning,

discovered God
was not the answer
but the mystery.
He thought some.
Later he committed
verse.
Then we knew
it had happened.

He is well now—
as well
as he will ever be—
except he sometimes
faces the corner
wall. Well,
he eats little.
He is clean and quiet.
And we've grown
used to him,
rather.

## EPITAPH

You, by an invention
of smiles, drove her mad.
She died quite mad.

You smiled and the sea
was born, a convoluted shell
that was her anguish.

Hours dropped their leaves
into her empty lap.
She waited, listening the sea.

She thanked you
for your gift, your shell.
Drifting off, you nodded.

The sea will swallow
your naked smile. No leaves
will shield your grave.

The sobbing has begun again.
Within the shell
the sea pursues its course.

# THE PRINCE MOURNS HIS LOVE

KISSING THE DRAGON GOOD-NIGHT
three years ago, I was amused
to note it turned into a Princess.

Come alive, I sang, you're
in the Pepsi Generation. She
was annoyed. A hundred years

in scales does the disposition
little good. She wanted not a song
but love. Love of a true Prince

had made her once again a Princess,
she maintained, and she was right.
I loved her. But I loved her

as the dragon she had been. I
was amused: the transformation
seemed unlikely to persist.

She raged. It made her mad
I loved the Princess less than
the enchanted dragon. She wished

the dragon's death. Because
she was again a true Princess,
she had her wish. The dragon died.

Days spun by upon her flaxen wheel
while she wept because I loved her
for her truest self. Three times

from violets to varnished leaves,
three times the disenchantment
of her humbled generation. Come

alive no more. The brass green
fire of her furious eyes grew dim.
She died upon my kiss in disbelief.

# III. The Death of Kings

# THE DEATH OF KINGS

for John F. Kennedy (1917–1963)

## I

WIT AND PASSION ARE ALLAYED
With ritual. The king must die.
They lead him to the pit arrayed
In gold. Death cowers in his eye.

They wash him for the sacrifice,
Anoint him with the sacred blood.
He stands and marvels their precise
Observance, kneads the crimson mud.

The double ax is raised. He thinks
He understands whatever dies:
Carrion on the altar stinks,
His sacred body swarms with flies.

Nerves cling desperate to bone
While murder probes the patient head
For entrance. Now his eyes are stone.
The ax is down. The king lies dead.

In three days they consume his flesh,
Or parts of it; the rest is burned.
They breathe again. The air is fresh
That feeds them gross and unconcerned.

## II

That blind imperative
of love
deceives.

We spy
beyond the eye's
idolatry

god
squinting in the good
smoke of the blood

and think
we please him. Rank
and thick

souls, we serve
our selves;
the hungry god starves.

Always so. The sacrifice begun
as worship ends in lust, the one
attempted good lost in confusion.

The king must die. A garden story
stirs in the mind, a memory
of some ancient blazing fury

when we chose not to be loved:
we shall be as gods and live
forever. We die and we forgive

our failure. Only the tainted seed
remains. We kill the living god
we cannot understand, being dead.

### III

There was this Jew, see, hung up
on love. I mean like love is
the whole action. Man, he swung—
a little too far out. We screwed him
to a cross. Faked out, Dad.

### IV

Dead, they told me. I went upstairs
and took off all my clothes, tried to wash
away his death. I stood, a stone beneath
the scalding water, incapable of tears.

There shudders in the secret heart
an eskimo who comes by night to ice-fields,
chops a tiny hole and sets his knife
to freeze, blade pointing at the crimson moon,
tip anointed with his hunter blood.
The handle fixes in the ice. Later,
wolves come slavering the blood,
lap the knife blade over,
over,
slit tongues running on the bloody steel.
They pour out blood, they gulp it down.
In the end they fall exsanguinated.
They die devouring themselves.

The heart rebels. Blood's brother
crying out from earth denies the end.
First comes knowledge that I am;
then the loneliness begins.

### V

In the hard eye of one quite casual day
a man of goodness died. He had foreseen
the possibility—"tall building, telescopic sight"—
no modest prophet came to warn the king.

These were the facts.
The air was washed in morning light when Love
Field took him and the motorcade began:
motorcycles, pilot car,
    motorcycles, lead car,
        presidential limousine,
            motorcycles, on and on,
with two unscheduled descents:
to shake a hand, to greet a nun and children.
Down Main Street to the cross with Houston,
north on Houston where the waiting crowds
cheered from shade of tall and patient buildings.

Where Houston crosses Elm they knew they loved him.

At 12:30 on Elm Street
while he was moving toward the Triple Underpass
a bullet shattered the right side of his skull.
His wife cradled him lifeless in her lap.

These were the facts.
And all the light of that quite casual day—gone.


VI

Life in the bright blood spilled
teaches us the art of dying, ritual
of love. Death is not the end, nor
violence, nor long dark passages of night.

The end is vision:
stones roll back and wonder cracks
like morning on a disbelieving world.
No Lazarus standing gray and stupid
in his linen bands, but we—harlequins
and fools—stride the fired air
with feet of bronze. Laughter
is our music. Let the earth tremble.

40

In full light of each ascending hour
we die and die. It is our token
of the numinous encounter, that last
surrender when we let ourselves be loved.

*IV. Certain Dangerous*
*Observations*

## THE LANDSCAPE

WHEN THE HILLS COLLAPSED, WE WENT INSIDE
the house and hated one another.
We listened while the frenzied wings
battered at the wind; waited, knees
against our chests.

And then the house collapsed. We lived
somehow. Summer that year was heavy
with bees, melting golden on the humming
branch; molten, orchid, sound of bronze.
Bees were the beginning.

They gave us honey and the law, taught us
how to hear the light wingbeat of love
behind the storm. We learned to bear with
one another, found new earth, wandered
in the garden of our flesh.

Hungry, I grow rich with loving, give
my love, am given more until the weighted
vines go down upon their knees and we see
evening sunlight on the hills. There is no
hunger like the taste of you.

# THE COMMAND

WHEN YOU ENTERED THE DARK TEMPLE
all the statues shook and fell.
They had not seen so beautiful a one.

The fall between your breasts and belly
was their hearts' plummet;
hawks dive and arabesque
the still sands shift to music of your flesh.

No hand will ever trace that line
that secret knowledge
of a death or fleshly paradise
but hearts know all forbidden territory
hawks are pitiless.

And mind
though it will not
stands erect and shakes the statues down.

Fall down.
Fall down before the flesh of my beloved.
I am there
and will not have strange gods before me.

# THE AGE OF FAVOURS

Ten penny nails in my tin Hedges box
are favours. I keep them. Because it's later
now than it has ever been before.
Private mystery unravels with the knowing.

She loved him, in the fairy tale, because
he loved her first for her white hands
and yellow hair. In time her hands did whiten
and her hair was summer flax. Later
as his eyes grew weak he loved her
that her face was plain. It always had been.
And at the end, when all his joy was watching
how the gulls dipped to the water
like toys on strings, he loved her railing
at him down the hours of his sleep
for all that he had never been. He settled
for the sorry best he was: imperfection
to the level of his love. He loved her.
That was a fact he sealed in a small chest,
never took out, never reconsidered. Its mystery
survived the long unravelling of knowledge.
Naked, inaccessible, it became her hands
and hair, caressed her questioning face,
discovered song and variation in her wrath.
Fact is the mystery; it survives.

The ten penny nails, the box, the cryptogram:
they help to stay the lateness of the hour.

## THE MASKED BALL

I

WE COME TO THE MASKED BALL
the poor poet and I as chimpanzee
and lion. Animals are certain:
metaphysics cloud not one
of their aggressions. They wear

upon the fuzzy face the heart's
cartography. Harpsichords jangle
in the air a melody that turns
and starts again before the sound
has heard itself quite out.

These are the odd geometries
of love: the masks of animals,
Vivaldi with a limp. And then
there is the new equation, death's
equality before the blade descends.

Masks come off; the certain hand
beckons from the open door; eyes,
hooded, blink the blade up while
the heart goes numb and the tongue
flaps stupid in the wild mouth.

Thud. The stricken head, cut
clean and at an angle, plops

into the basket. Costume, music
for a ritual dance. We wear the livery
of our calling: lion, chimpanzee.


2

The gods of blood drink bowls of milk and roses.
Altars flow with perfect sacrifice, the hissing
milk, the rose on fire. Death is their laughter.

Animals their prey, unlettered beasts who bleed
and wail but do not question masks or butterflies
or nine month's tasking. Banquets are their honor.

The gods of blood wear masks of rope and silver.
Let the hornet moon come buzzing, sting closed
the hundred eyes of gods and poets, stain

the milk, rape the rose, drown golden in a pool
of blood. Masks. The gods of blood live on.
The god of wine and crusts forever comes, is

coming all ways. At a distance down the dusty
road, trees embrace a crossing and he comes;
he comes in fever and in gallows and in love.


3

Swing your partner
round and back

meet at night
behind the shack

go for a little walk
back for a little talk

turn, return, and promenade
first serve mammon

then serve god
dozey-do and doozey-doo

you scratch me
and I'll scratch you.

We stand aside, then close, and then embrace.

And still we are no closer. Time and music
cannot mend the ragged tear, the fraying

edges of a simple trust. The gods of blood
with bowls of milk and roses seek oblivion.

The harpsichord records their bland despair.

How put together what the knife has cut?
How make the parallel of love a single arc?

The soul grows sick of groaning for fulfillment
and the sweating dancers do not hear him come.

Make a little bow
now ain't she pretty

show her how
she's from the city

swing your partner
left then right

sun's gone down
and the moon's not bright

duck for the oyster
dig for the clam

it's jellyroll time
so let's make jam.

4

Give me one shell one curious rock glittering
with chips of rain or veined with flywings, then
I will follow. Some magpie matter, something

I can hold in mind if not in hand, turn over,
weigh. There are animals in veins of stone
and human profiles merging beasts grotesque

enough for an apocalypse—this too in time—
and hills and brooks and battlements and eyes
of fevered mercenaries marching down long

centuries to glory, conquest, rape: service
of the fatherland. Stones will cry out.
Stones and masks: in chaos, patterns of some

midnight hope cling bone and clay, arrest
the awful hour. It is time. The world's
night hovers in these tangled branches. Come.


5

Harpsichords are not enough.
Metaphysics of the heart require
a word to strip away the mask,
to strike between the dance
and music, bare animal and blood.

His language is the eye's gesture,
foot tapping to the quickened pulse,
timely motion toward an absolute.
Peaches heavy on the gilded branch;
the tree that flowered every year

and gave in all its life one stunted
dessicated plum; grapes purple,
bursting on the vine. Fertile, barren,

stunted: trees are a language. And
that other more uncomfortable tree.

We dance as chimpanzee and lion,
fulfill the ritual of harpsichord
and knife and metaphysics. We dance
and I recall I saved the plum almost
twenty days; it did not rot; it withered

smaller. That mortal knot remains.
The dance is danced, the blade
is sharpened, the bloody head thuds dead
into the basket. Geometry of love.
And still the word forever comes.

# V. Exploring the Gallery

# TO A FRIEND CONTEMPLATING SUICIDE

STILL YOU REFUSE TO LEAP.
Think the quarry—stone cut out
and carried off—is a gaping

hospitable womb. And leap.
Then we will love you, swathe
your broken life with bandages

of flowers. We will love you.
I am courageous as most
and know with granite certainty

I would have leaped long since.
Death becomes easy when life
is so meticulous with grief.

Who is your god, I wonder?
What strange stone desires this?
Leap. Leap or despite my god

I swear I'll push you
to your death. Guilt is less
painful than the ruins of your eyes.

## A PLEASING FRAGRANCE

HE WAS CROWING
on the rooftop
of his sanctity

when the house burned
down. Crazy old cock
larger than death

he thought
before the conflagration.
It *was* a fire, though,

noise and apparatus
and he up there
coining phrases

with his tail in flames.
He would have laughed
to see himself.

Maybe he did laugh.
Maybe that was why
he crowed,

because he knew
it was preposterous
and wanted to go out

the way he'd lived.
And so he's gone,
poor roasted soul,

in blazing glory.
He made, despite himself,
a good holocaust.

## AMBIGUITIES OF WAITING

A HOLLOW HEAD IS LITTLE PROOF
   against uncertainty. For burial
   nothing is too good. If you
   follow me. If you follow me,

of course, we might confound
   Marvell who knew a thing or more
   about the grave. We might wake
   nights and walk by pallid light

of marvelous stars or lie twined
   in tight embrace, with our
   whispers waking the infelicitous
   dead. Or we might not. For

it is said there are no marriages
   in heaven. (Might it be that
   stones are the fulfillment
   and bridges only dreams?)

We could inquire the wise, but
   Thomas, my life, is very long
   and love, alas, is short. Let
   us revel in our timely grave.

## HALF A SONNET

I SHALL SING YOU A LOVE SONG IN SEVEN LINES.

When you spoke, the birds of spring committed
suicide, seeing their futility in song.
When you walked, the brooks despaired
your motion, slowed to rivulets, dried up.
And when you folded your small heart
within my own, I too died at your giving.
I leave you. I need the dark of imperfection.

Seven lines and seven years have passed.
Today I saw a swallow at the meadow brook
and wondered, did I really love you? Ever?

## NARCISSUS

I AM WITTY AND WELL-WASHED.
I know five languages, speak
three reasonably well. My features
are strong but not offensive.
Golden mediocrity.

Once by the water, it is true,
I paused unconscionably long,
grew thin as ragweed, scraggly,
got strange habits of the mind.
That was a phase.

Now I spend my eyes watching
for the tall stranger who knew me
through the water, loved who
I might have been. I drown each
morning, nameless.

## LINES TO BE RECITED
## WHILE BURNING AT THE STAKE

I KNOW
some things.

Love corrupts
slower
than knowledge
faster
than flesh.

Choices
we make
destroy us
when they are
unselfish.

Death
is the end.
I know
I love you
no longer.

I choose death.
For myself.

# AT THE RELUCTANT BAR AND GRILL

THE HEART IS BOUGHT.
We understand at once
and miss the point,

nodding agreement
summoning the name that trips
too facile off the tongue.

No good. The heart is bought
now and will love
no more. Drink will do

you in, they said.
It didn't. Nor did lesions.
Nor swiss cheese I use for skin.

It was other things.
The found father
and the undiscovered self

are one.
That was something.
But mostly the bought heart.

I shall summon no sacred names,
sign no agreement. I shall sit—
pounding an occasional table—

and contemplate rhinoceri
in knickers. Rhinoceri will love
no more. The heart is bought.

After this fashion,
and with a little luck,
we survive.

## THE FRIEND

His IRONY WAS EPITAPH
for his emotions. They died
one night of a slight chill
and a long cold rain.

After that he loved
with caution, testing time
and weather and direction
of the wind. He waited.

Seasons grew and bloomed
and faded into ash; his wit
became his countenance. He
smiled wryly, spoke in epigrams.

He never hurt. His charm,
his bland ironic stance,
put us at ease and gave us
everything—except himself.

With all his friends
it was a mystery he died
alone. Later we remembered
we had never heard him laugh.

## *IN HARBOR*

WE THINK WE SWIM; BUT THE TIDE
knows who swims and who is borne.

Birth is something other. Flesh parts
and we are forced, unwelcome, on the small

mercy of our lovers. They try to give
only the best gifts, only saving graces,

but the apple rots and even carnations
wither. That fiber of our love, we find,

is straw not steel. The molten heart
becomes a brief and startled flame

consuming self. We are our darkness
proper. Wholeness asks this birth

by fire: each day's death of love.
Ashes sometimes drift against the tide.

# A SUFFICIENCY OF WOMEN

WOMEN—WHEN THEY CEASE TO BE SOFT MICE—
are brilliant feathered birds or animals
or tropic rains. They happen: total,
without warning. I have known five.

Adria lived on spring rain and violets;
a clean small animal with dainty claws
she washed her food, fastidious, in the stream.
(she washed my heart and left it on the bank)
The scent of violets went with her.

Carla was half lion, half flamingo,
fabled creature from a mythic time
when goddesses made love to mortal men.
(she will live and live by the moon's shadow)

Katherine was English sunrise in December;
burred, astringent, in the white cold dawn.
(her grace is hard and permanent as truth)

Laura was a sparrow, wounded, broken.
(who would have thought that, dying,
she could turn her head upon her wing
and plunge her bill beneath my seventh rib?)

Joan was bird and beast and season: blackbird
whirring in the snow, stark extremes
of porpentine whose only quills are love,

my soul's own strict and various weather.
She is altogether free; without parentheses.

Women never wholly die; they tease
the elements to preserve their one fantastic
gift, survive all weather of the heart.
Five women are enough. I die wealthy.

# VI. The Problem of God

# SIX VARIETIES OF RELIGIOUS EXPERIENCE

"If in 'Velvet Shoes' Elinor Wylie had
written 'Let us put on appropriate
galoshes' there could, of course, have
been no poem."
    —heard in a poetry lecture

LET US PUT ON APPROPRIATE GALOSHES
and thrash about in the snow. Lodgers
do that and we are, after all, only

thirty. I shall lie down (carefully)
on my back, flash my arms in geometric
arcs, and make an angel. You can build

a snowman. (You are always constructive)
We grow old and parenthetical: propriety
encloses us like boots, like sensible

shoes, like foot-formers wrenching waxy
bones to necessary shape. Let us pitch
rigidity to hell, not think what they

might say. Let us put on appropriate
galoshes, floppy ones that fill with snow.
Let us risk wet feet and colds and madness.

When we lie abed (like skunks, you know,
snug in their trees when the snow whistles)
we shall smile and say: well, *that* was good.

## THE LAST VEIL

THE SISTER DYING
hurled her crucifix across the room.

Nuns rustled their unlikely beads.
Beads rattled in their wooden hands.

She is mad,
they said, and prayed more firmly.
So many years faithful to his mind.

Screaming hate
she flailed him from her bed, shook
her wild hair against his words.

She died refusing. Spared forever
that sterile heaven she had loathed,

she woke
astonished to her unexpected lover.

# THREE AWFUL PICNICS

(as told to *Time* magazine by his widow)


I

WHEN HIS HEAD SPLIT OPEN LIKE A ROTTEN
cantaloupe and seven birds flew out,
we were surprised. We fell silent.
You don't expect a thing like that—
not even on a weekend in the country.

He muttered, bubbling from his split
left mouth: "Christ, I'm schizo now
for real." His sense of humor was appalling.
I recall we raised our eyes deliberately
and watched the seven birds describe
the circle of descending day, fly back
to consciousness again, again. We
memorized their flaming throats, their cries.
How long until we can forget this place?

His suit was ruined. So was our cookout.
We gathered up the picnic things
and left at once. Walking to the cars,
his friend remarked to me, concerned:
"Well, he's never done *that* before."


2

He had been trying to imagine God. Still,
when his head split open like a cantaloupe

and three brown birds flew out, we were
surprised. One two three. Sure enough.
There they were: like a judgment.

"Only who are loved are capable of loving,"
he used to say, though he himself
never seemed the kind to die for love
let alone to split in two for it. We knew
about his thing with God only when he told us.
Counted measured prayed watched: he had
done it all, scrubbed his patience to a gloss,
finally lost interest in God. Resented him.
Resented God's impervious omnipotence, love
computerized and lavished on the hateful,
impossible demands of law. He lived his death.

So when his head split open and birds spilled
to the sky, he would have thought it judgment.
Perhaps it was. Certainly there *were*
three birds. But he was not the kind for that;
never the religious type, really.


### 3

Nature ceased to war with grace in him.
Sometimes when that melon has released
its sparrow, appearances will shift and what is
will be revealed; decision will evoke response.
So when, after we had passed the wine, his head
split open and five green birds flew out,
we were less surprised. We half expected it.
He always seemed the kind to die in public.

He had spoken often of his name. "No one
knew it," he said, "no one ever would."
No hands tender on his secret body,
exploring hidden reaches of knowledge and desire.
No lips upon his eyelids blind from the light.

No total knowledge ever; his name unknown.
He talked like that, a little overwrought.

Still he made a good death. Undertakers
fixed his head so—except up close—you'd never
guess what happened. The birds return
sometimes in spring. Then we think of him
and his odd ways. He was wrong, however.
We all remember his name.

## CAIN

Yes, I have refused
to let God be.

He smiled
and smiled
at what he thought
I was
until I took a stone
and smashed his yellow eyes.

Now I go
into my room
(pull the world in behind me)
and slam the door.

## THE BARGAIN

"GIVE BACK MY CAT
and I'll believe in God."

She was mad, poor lady.
But sane enough to strike

a proper bargain. Then
someone—a priest—gave

her a cat which she loved
half to death for a month

trading it finally for
the apple core from Eden,

another patient exchange.
She misses the cat now,

cannot explain her trade.
"Blame God, his jealousy."

She weeps faithfully
mourning her lost cat.

## GOD, DYING

NOTHING BORES LIKE THE WORD OF GOD
made grammar: blunted reeds rammed
into our ears—not shaken by the wind
but rattled in an angry hand that knows
no gentle touch. No soft animal warms
beneath it, no seed grows to promise.

Once in the cave meat sizzled on the stone.
It was good. Smells of roasting flesh
summoned quaking bellies to the sacred feast.
The mind shudders as teeth strike living bone.

We have left the cave for good. The sacred
slaughterhouse that smelled of roasting flesh
is gone. The flesh is gone—out of our lives,
out of the summons to the living feast.
We pick among dead bones beneath fluorescent
light, bore into the grammar of the truth.

## CELEBRATION

VOICES OF THE VENGEFUL DEAD CURSE
in the leaves sometimes. In autumn they do.
The smiling corpse reflects upon old hate.

I never left the rains of my deluge—
forty days of drowning. After that
blight clung to my clothes like burrs.

Courage and the creeping damp ached
in the branches and the roots; uncertainty
caught at my hands as I passed by.

Suicide solved nothing. I knew
it wouldn't and so I didn't fight
recovery. And then my faith returned.

Everything will wither in the end.
But have you ever died before, they said.
Only on the greater feasts, I said.

## PERICHORESIS AND THE SINGLE SEMINARIAN

1 *The Streetcleaner*

THE SKY IS FALLING!
The sky is falling!
Relax, it's always falling.
Thirty-two years I'm sweeping
blue glass. I know
it's falling. My back,
see, I can't straighten it
I've been sweeping sky so long.
Some old eyes
a sneer
an unused idea
a broken chihuahua
one day a piece of God—
scared the hell out of me—
you find anything.
Now if you'll move please,
Mister, you're standing
on some sky.
So would you, Mister.
All right, the sky is falling!
So tell God.
So get a lawyer.

2 *The Trouble with Epiphanies*

Christ came into my room
and stood there

and I was bored to death.
I had work to do.
I wouldn't have minded
if he'd been crippled
or something—I do well
with cripples—but he
just stood there, all face,
and with that damned guitar.
I didn't ask him to sit down:
he'd have stayed all day.
(Let's be honest. You
can be crucified just so often;
then you've had it. I mean
you're useless; no good
to God, let alone
to anybody else.) So I said
to him after a while—
well, what's up? what do you want?
And he laughed, stupid,
said he was just passing by
and thought he'd say hello.
Great, I said, hello.
So he left.
And I was so damned mad
I couldn't even listen
to the radio. I went
and got some coffee.
The trouble with Christ is
he always comes at the wrong time.


3 *Hazards of Intimacy*

There was this pigeon, see,
a big bastard
flopping around my ears
and I thought Geez
I'll catch it in the eye
and be as blind as Tobey.

I mean I don't see
so great anyway—
but blind
I don't need it.
So in a couple days
this pigeon settles
and he's kind of peaceful.
I stop worrying
about his in-flight habits.
I give him hamburg
now and then,
some peanutbutter sandwich
Fridays (I'm Catholic;
let the Pope eat meat on Friday;
damned if I will)
and he lets me feed him
and gargle at him
like I was a pigeon too
if you know what I mean.
And it's nice. We belong.
We're friends, sort of.
So on last Monday,
two months I'm feeding him now,
he's sitting under a parked car
that starts to move.
I make a dive for him
(so God is dying?)
and grab him by the wing
and save him (only his wing
gets broken). I lose
three fingers of my right hand.
Cut right off.
Zing. Like that.
I can see all right. I just
can't feel anything.
Three fingers. He's a nice
pigeon though.